Simple Words of a Complex Man

Kevin Schwartzberg

Kevin Schwartzberg

Copyright © 2019 **Kevin Schwartzberg**
Cover Art © 2019 **Kevin Schwartzberg**
Editor: **Ashley Jane**

Kevin Schwartzberg
Illinois, USA

All rights reserved. No part of this publication may be reproduced, distributed, or transmitted in any form or by any means, without prior written permission, unless for the purposes of reviewing.

Author's Note: This is a work of fiction. Locales and public names are sometimes used for atmospheric purposes. Any resemblance to actual people, living or dead, or to businesses, companies, events, institutions, or locales are completely coincidental.

Simple Words of a Complex Man/
Kevin Schwartzberg 1st Edition
ISBN 978-0-578-46514-2

To all who have been
a part of my journey:

Some of you broke me down.
Some of you lifted me up.
But together,
we made the man before you today.
Simple in words, but complex in heart.

Above all others, to my son,
you have taught me what it is
to love unconditionally
and what strength really looks like.

Contents

Introduction	5
Simply Dying	9
The Complexity of Living	63
Words of A Man	123
Acknowledgements	185
About the Author	186

Introduction

Kevin Schwartzberg is the perfect example of how to turn pain into grace and poetry. He pens pain through words borrowed from hell and shines the light at the end of the tunnel to show the only way out is through, and he always comes out the other side as though hell never got a good grip on him. His light casts a shadow across pain, and we are all lucky enough to burn in the flames of his words; bright and tender, yet hard and sure like the one explosion we run to.

- Stephanie Bennett-Henry

Kevin Schwartzberg's writing invites you to climb his limbs, feel his roots in this earth, and absorb how nature has impacted his writing therapy. His book, Simple Words of a Complex Man, is the must read poetry book of the year. It is a debut collection of complex emotions stemming from a heart grafted by pain.

His lines are the poetic elixir for the woes that gnaw at defeated spirits. His carefully chosen words are healing, and they will boldly knock on your heart's door begging you to ask questions. And, as he tries to understand his own shipwrecked emotions, we journey along, gaining insight into our own search for peace.

Chivalry is not dead.

It still exists, and it lives inside the Simple Words of a Complex Man.

- Alfa Holden, author of Abandoned Breaths

Rarely have I read poetry or prose quite as lovely and entirely accessible as Kevin's. Without relying on the flowery imagery and over-the-top words that far too many modern poets overuse, Kevin is able to connect with his readers on a soul level by simply speaking from his heart. Simple Words of A Complex Man is anything but simple: it is raw, and it is true, it is hard, and it is sharp, it is beautiful, and it is painful, and it is everything we've all come to feel during our lives. It's just written far better than anything we've ever known. I am in love with this masterpiece.

- Nicole Lyons, author of The Lithium Chronicles

A gripping debut poetry book with the feel of a seasoned writer, Kevin is undeniably a power house with words, turning heartache into flames - "You will not smother this light." It is refreshing to read vulnerability from a man's perspective. He offers us a gift of hope, strength and redemption though his intuitive, healing ink in Simple Words of a Complex Man. Kevin's unique style will leave the reader hungry and eager for more, rest assured. Praise for this new voice on the poetry circuit.

- *Melody Lee, author of Moon Gypsy*

Hey there
Come on in
Take a seat
Don't worry
Every seat is a good seat
Welcome to the shit show

Kevin Schwartzberg

Simply Dying

Kevin Schwartzberg

They say if you find yourself in a hole
Just stop digging
Sounds so simple
But what do you do...
If no matter how hard you try
You just can't let go of the shovel

Simple Words of a Complex Man

Am I the only one who feels this way
Weakened and weary from the struggle
How can one man be an army
I have to believe you would understand
Whoever you are
There is so much more to this life
There has to be...
We have not laughed enough
I haven't felt your embrace
Yet I know without a doubt
Together, we would be unstoppable
If only I didn't have to fast forward
Through the autobiography of my life
Desperate to find your name in the credits

Kevin Schwartzberg

The water slowly rises
Keeping steady pace with my panic
I feel the pressure on my chest
The burning in my lungs
The weight of the world on my shoulders
Pushing me deeper and deeper
Closer to everlasting peace
I have known all along I was drowning
But I always believed
I was holding you above the water
Only to now realize
It was you pushing me under

Every fucking time

Here is my heart
Please be kind
I hope... no I pray
You will use it wisely

So why am I surprised
To find myself neck deep
Suffocating in emotional concrete
Brick by brick
Building that wall a little higher

On your way out the door
Please
Do not forget to leave your
Handprints in the mortar of my soul
If you can find room

Kevin Schwartzberg

You choose yourself
Time and time again
Words and actions
In direct opposition
Skillfully blending fact and fiction
So lost in deceit
You eventually believe
Your own narcissistic bullshit
Fortunately for you
The innocence of youth
Prevents him from seeing
The truth behind your lies
But one day soon
It will be your turn to cry
Way too little...way too late
He will be a grown man
Obligatory love will be dead
Unrequited devotion absent
Replaced by the knowledge
You exist only for yourself
And always have

Simple Words of a Complex Man

Chapped cracked skin
Lips stained with blood
Come drink from my well
Fill your aching soul again
While I slowly die
Of dehydration

Kevin Schwartzberg

I should stand
I should run
I should scream
Do something for god's sake
But instead
I am here
On hands and knees
The dirt and mud
Churned red with blood
My shattered black soul finally defeated
Vacant eyes staring upon
What is left of the battlefield

Simple Words of a Complex Man

I remember the exact instant
The taste in the back of my throat
The sickly sweet smell on the wind
Lying in the grass
Staring at the sky
Struggling to catch my breath
My heart barely contained
Trying to burst free of my chest
All the while only one vision
Clear in my mind
You

Kevin Schwartzberg

Nights like this
Devour my soul
Twist my mind
Make me wonder
What if the lesser of two evils
Was actually
Being completely alone while
Sharing the same bed

Simple Words of a Complex Man

Everyone knows
Monsters live in the shadows
I suppose that explains
Why yours
Reside in your heart

Kevin Schwartzberg

A shadow of myself
I am an empty vessel
That will never float
With holes that cannot be patched
I will never grasp
How you derived
Such pleasure from
Grinding my soul
Beneath your soles

Kevin Schwartzberg

Cheap words
Are like cheap silver
Both tarnish quickly
And leave you green

Simple Words of a Complex Man

I see you talking
Your mouth moving
A series of words strung together
Emphasized by the fire in your eyes
I'm sure if I could stop and breathe
Absorb the words together
Their combined meaning
Then maybe I would understand
But I hear them individually
Word...By...Word
Devoid of any meaning
The only thing I feel is
Warm air slapping me in the face
Escaped from the shackles of your mind
Delivered from your lips
Instead
I'm staring past you
At the man in the mirror
Wondering who he is
And when he stole my life

Kevin Schwartzberg

You are
The vacancy in my heart
My plus one that will never arrive
My soul mate that will never be
I will never let go of hope
I will never give up on us
And I will continue to suffer in silence
So that you may live in bliss

Simple Words of a Complex Man

It's what I have always done
I knew no other way
Everyone else came first
I rejected the very concept of
Putting on my oxygen mask first
Before helping those around me
No...I would be the one to suffocate
As I held your mask in place
It's taken me many deaths
Many sleepless nights
But I have finally learned
In completely sacrificing myself
For the sake of another
We both end up empty

Kevin Schwartzberg

No matter how many times
I replay it in my mind
Trust me I have...
I feel the sting of each word
And the accompanying tears
Over and over again
The outcome is the same
Hurt from every angle
I can only hope that
What was once beautiful
Has not forever changed
Into what I feel tonight
Because I am truly terrified
Of what life looks like
Without you in it

Simple Words of a Complex Man

I will never forget the moment
When my conscious mind accepted
What my heart had known for ages
You will never love me
The way that I love you
And the warmth inside
Turned bitter and died

Kevin Schwartzberg

There is no way to make it right
So it seems this is goodbye
I didn't think it could hurt any worse
When my heart already breaks
Every fucking day
But trust me when I tell you
It can ...
I will never again
Underestimate the torture of
Being able to only love
A portion of someone

Lesson learned
Never tempt the universe
I assure you
It can always be worse
It can always hurt more
You can always feel
Even more alone
Than you did one hour before
No amount of tears
Can undo this pain
And rebuild my shattered heart

Kevin Schwartzberg

The bitter truth it seems
Is the only real break we get
From our daily struggles
Are the ones we create ourselves
So revel in the silence
Smile in absolute darkness
Find peace in your chaos
And be kind to yourself
Always

Simple Words of a Complex Man

How come the only thing we can agree upon
Is that this isn't the way it's supposed to be
Your words cut deep
But your actions
They know the way to my heart
No door can slow them
They ignore the walls I have built
They are on a mission and will not be swayed
They steal my breath and twist my guts
Do you even know me at all
Do you realize I wear pain
Like a sweatshirt in a rain storm
It seems like it magically disappears
But let me assure you
EVERY FUCKING DROP
Is being absorbed
Soaking in
Adding weight to my already
Over laden soul
Chilling me to the bone

Kevin Schwartzberg

For years I played your games
A willing participant
Of my own eventual demise
Ignorant of what narcissism even was
Let alone the feminine curves it wore
Occasional glimpses of freedom and happiness
Only to be drawn back in
Wondering what I did wrong
Again
Always desperate to make it right
Knowing in my heart
I could never actually fix what was broken
Within you

Simple Words of a Complex Man

Tears run down my cheek
Still the words won't come
Even if I could find them
You wouldn't understand
Nobody really does
I would gladly give you my shoes
If you would care to walk in them
Then perhaps you wouldn't be so quick to judge
To armchair quarterback my life
My decision and my pain
We certainly wouldn't want that
No, nobody said it would be easy
But they could have told me
It would be this fucking hard

Kevin Schwartzberg

12:53 and I can't sleep
Again
I'm home alone in an empty house
An empty bed
I wish you were in both my home
And my arms tonight
Well every night actually
All the hurt and all the pain
Every bad decision
They have all led me to this point
This time in my life
And to you

Simple Words of a Complex Man

It feels like flipping a switch
One minute you are here
The next you are gone
The lights didn't slowly fade
They just ceased to exist
I blinked and you were gone
No time for reflection
No time for goodbyes

Kevin Schwartzberg

You want to know
Do I still miss you
Only the softness of your lips
As they pressed into my soul
The feeling of your hand
Interlaced with my spirit
The sound of your laughter
Gently caressing my mind
The constant butterflies
When our eyes would meet
And the excitement every day brought
Knowing you would be a part of it
Perhaps a better question is
How can I learn to breathe without you

Simple Words of a Complex Man

I am terrified of the dark
Not of things that go bump in the night
I think I would even welcome their company
But when the lights turn off
My mind turns on
There is no escaping the reality
Of how alone I actually feel
And the staggering pain of solitude

Kevin Schwartzberg

You robbed my spirit
Stole my time
Left my soul bankrupt
My interest void
You broke me
And the cost of words unspoken
Is more than my heart can afford
You should have told me
Your love was on loan
Then I would have expected
It to be gone
When I needed it most

Simple Words of a Complex Man

When all the hurtful words
Are said and done and
The tears have dried
I remember the way it felt
When things were simple
A boy loved a girl
That was all we needed
Those days are long gone
All I have left
Are memories and heartache
The only thing left to say is
........goodbye

Kevin Schwartzberg

I tried for years to forget the past
Swallow the pain and fight the loneliness
Only to eventually admit defeat
Accepting the most difficult lesson
I have ever had to learn
Regardless of how bad you want it
No matter how hard you are trying
Fighting and clawing and screaming
Sometimes love just isn't enough
Not by a long shot

Simple Words of a Complex Man

Its 2:20 and I am chasing shadows
Shadows on the wall
Shadows in my heart
Memories of what should have been
Memories of what could have been
Sometimes when I least expect it
Emotion seeps through my barricades
Real emotion
The shit that completely fucks me up
The past has taught me 100%
Emotion is a package deal
Inclusive of pain and heartache
Sometimes what you need to say the most
Is just impossible to express in words
I've been told speaking your demons' names
Will render them powerless
But let me assure you
They still have power
Only difference is now they know
That I am fucking terrified of them

Kevin Schwartzberg

Don't you dare
Apologize for making me cry
It's the only real emotion
I feel anymore
And probably the only honest thing
You have ever done to me
This I know
This is my wheelhouse
I find comfort in the pain
If you were to make me smile
Now **that** would be truly terrifying

Simple Words of a Complex Man

I would rather feel this devastation
Time and time again
Than to feel nothing at all

Kevin Schwartzberg

Sometimes
You feel just like a dream
Existing only in my mind
On the other side of these words
Always finding the hidden significance
That eludes even me
You speak to both my heart and mind
Without actually speaking at all
Such an undeniable raw connection
Yet devoid of any physical connection
It can only leave me questioning
Everything and everyone
Before this moment
If this is in fact a dream
I pray I never wake

Simple Words of a Complex Man

Pain or pleasure
Pleasure or pain
Choose carefully for
Eventually they both
Become the same
And we will settle
For either
If only it'll save us
From the shallow monotony
Of everyday life

Kevin Schwartzberg

The problem is I ultimately
Started to believe the bullshit
That I wasn't good enough
No matter what I did
Or how hard I tried
That would never change
It was a powerful day when I finally realized
One person cannot love enough
To offset the emotional vacancy of another
And even the darkest night
Can be defeated by the smallest spark

One person cannot bear the weight
Of another's existence
While maintaining their own

Simple Words of a Complex Man

I have never walked away from a challenge
Never been one to easily admit defeat
But my heart and my will
Are at an impasse this time
What do you do
When there is no outcome
That does not end in heartache
And the challenge itself
Is to simply walk away

Kevin Schwartzberg

Relationships change
For better or worse
Some grow apart
Others grow together
But you and I
We have always been apart
Either never caring
Or learning to connect
I only wish it hadn't taken
Years of emotional turmoil
To finally realize this
And put you in my past

Simple Words of a Complex Man

Now I lay me down to sleep
If only it were that simple
As I lay here waiting for clarity
To questions I haven't even asked yet
I hear every sound
Normally masked by the noise of the day
The clock screams every passing minute
Daring me to drift off to sleep and miss a moment
Of the story it has yet to tell
While the fan has finally stopped groaning
Submitting to its monotonous fate of
Spinning in circles but never getting anywhere
Now I will spend the rest of the night
Wondering which one I am
The clock or the fan

Kevin Schwartzberg

Haunted
By the sound
Of laughter
Echoing off the walls
Of my hollow heart

Simple Words of a Complex Man

This is the loudest silence
I have ever heard
The deafening cacophony
Of my own breaking heart
Hammering away in my vacant chest
The darkness taunts me
And even the crickets harmonize
To sing of my misery

Kevin Schwartzberg

A direct connection
To that void in my chest
My eyes always speak the truth
Unable to filter the anguish
My mind so cleverly disguises
Before it escapes my mouth
I try to hide the fear
The years of disappointment
In myself and others
Only to be betrayed again and again
By scar lines left
From saline sorrow

Simple Words of a Complex Man

I thought I was alone by choice
Something I didn't fully comprehend
Until there was you
Now I find myself alone again
Missing your presence
A stranger to myself
The lone survivor
Of my heart's massacre

Kevin Schwartzberg

Constant pain changes us
Both physically and emotionally
We long for an escape
A position to ease the suffering
Or a pill that dulls the knife
When all the while
It slowly devours our souls

Simple Words of a Complex Man

Relationships often end
Long after they should have
Finally allowing us the clarity
To open previously locked doors
To destroy indestructible walls
Paving the way for new feelings
Through this pain we can achieve
Unimaginable growth and perspective
If we only allow ourselves the chance

Kevin Schwartzberg

I found peace in the darkness
Where emotional walls crumble
Carefully built façades deteriorate
Nobody can see the silent tears
Or hear the salty anguish
The world seems simple...
If only for a moment

Simple Words of a Complex Man

My heart is tired
My soul is spent
But I am at peace with life
And the darkness
That has consumed it
After years of confusion
I have finally realized
Even in the blackest darkness
Exists the promise of light
And I have learned to love the nighttime

Kevin Schwartzberg

Every ounce of pain
Feels like a million pounds
Every day alone seems
Longer and harder than the day before
The moment is now
Time to dig deep
Stop feeling sorry for yourself
Because no one else does
Be grateful for what you have
Be kind to those who don't deserve kindness
Find the beauty and happiness
In each and every moment you can
Never forget
It's the pain that allows us
To define the happiness

Kevin Schwartzberg

The Complexity of Living

Kevin Schwartzberg

I am now more certain than ever before
The universe is always communicating with us
The difficulty is silencing your own inner voice
Long enough to hear what is being said

Simple Words of a Complex Man

Warm summer nights
Tangled within cool breezes
Crisp smelling air
Cleansed by torrential downpours
Frigid winter mornings
Warm breath escaping your lungs
Fire colored leaves littering the ground
Unshackled from their wooden keepers

Kevin Schwartzberg

    Hopefully
Hope   fully
 A little space
  Can make a
   World of
   Difference
     In
     So
    Many
    Ways

Kevin Schwartzberg

Beauty surrounds us everywhere
If we could only slow down
Breathe
And focus upon
The splendor contained within the madness

Simple Words of a Complex Man

The actual stakes we play for
Are love and hate
Devotion and indifference
I wish it were as simple
As life and death

Kevin Schwartzberg

There comes a time in all our lives
Where you have to throw caution to the wind
Open the door and dance in the rain
No umbrella
No coat
Just you and the rain
Go ahead and cry
No one can tell the difference
But realize eventually
That same rain will wash away your pain

Simple Words of a Complex Man

Why do we feel it is acceptable
To use intimacy as a pawn
A means to an end
A gateway to materialistic greed

Kevin Schwartzberg

We are constantly finding new ways
To cause pain and sorrow to others
Instead of applying the same effort
To elevate the spirit of our fellow man
Once again I can only shake my head
In disgust

Simple Words of a Complex Man

I can't even remember the last time
I closed my eyes and found peace
I am beyond exhausted
To the point that simply tired
Would be an absolute vacation
My chest never stops pounding
My thoughts are always racing
Sleep is sporadic at best
Only serving as a temporary break
Between the moments of ambiguity
And utterly terrifying lucidity

Kevin Schwartzberg

Trust is a cruel mistress
And this bitch will teach you
The error of your ways
Time and time again
While you sit in the corner
Head in your hands
Helplessly watching her laugh
At the indistinguishable pieces
Of your heart and tears
As they combine
To make pain angels in the mud

Simple Words of a Complex Man

Intense pain

Hides

Behind **powerful** words

Kevin Schwartzberg

Life has proven to me
Over and over again
Given the right circumstances
Even an anchor can float
Repeatedly forcing me to question
The spiritual consequences
Of doing the wrong thing
Believing it's for the right reasons

Simple Words of a Complex Man

Am I broken
Am I bruised
Questions I continue to ask
Answers I'm not sure I want
Decisions made over and over
Playing narcissistic games
Cleverly disguised as love
They haunt my future
They poisoned my past
Regret...fuck yes
But it will not define me
My kindness will shine through
You will not smother this light

Kevin Schwartzberg

What you call cowardice
I call self-preservation
What you casually refer to as ignorance
I know to be careful strategy
You would be remiss to think
My unwillingness to cause turmoil
For all these years
Is in any way commensurate
To my acceptance of your behavior
Have no doubt that when the time comes
I am more than ready to fight this battle
This life is a game of chess
I have planned my moves in advance
I am more than prepared to sacrifice the pawns
In order to save the king

Simple Words of a Complex Man

I used to think opposites attract
Some sort of magnetic pull
They are drawn to us
We are drawn to them
I felt helpless to resist so why try
After years of devastation and heartache
Losing myself over and over again
Always putting my needs second
I have finally realized
Nature rarely deviates
They may have amazing camouflage
But I have learned to read the signs
I choose not to be preyed upon

Kevin Schwartzberg

Then there are days
There is no doubt
You are as real as my warm breath
Escaping into the cold crisp dawn
While the sky paints breathtaking sunrises
That only we can see
The breeze that reluctantly surrenders
The scent of your perfume
But only to me...
Making me weak in the knees
I frantically change the music
But it's no use
Every song sings the words
You gently whispered in my ear
I hear you as clearly
As the heart pounding in my chest
These are the days I am terrified
To close my eyes

Kevin Schwartzberg

Trust is a gift
Not given easily
And all too often
Returned in tatters

Simple Words of a Complex Man

When I was a young boy
My father taught me
You can't be mad at a panther
For having a black shadow
Anymore than at a snake
For having fangs
It is their nature
Not malicious intent
This leaves me questioning why
I cannot forgive you
For having both

Kevin Schwartzberg

The human condition dictates
We believe not only what we choose to
But what we NEED to
However the often brutal reality of life
Continues to prove to me
Over and over
Ignorance in fact can be bliss
And the truth doesn't always
Set you free

Simple Words of a Complex Man

There is no greater anguish
Than seeing your child in agony
Knowing there isn't enough hugs
Knowing there isn't enough words
No magic pills
That will end his pain
I have to be strong for us both
When all I want to do is cry with you
I would gladly take your place
If only I could
But for now my son
All I can do is hold your hand
And never let go
Together
We will ride out this storm

Kevin Schwartzberg

Tonight everything feels different
The midnight breeze pushes onward
Until it caresses my very soul
The slight scent of honeysuckle
Brings calm to my racing mind
I don't ever remember the stars
Shining quite this bright
My past will no longer haunt me
You will no longer haunt me
I earned these fucking scars
I will wear them like a badge
Warning others I am not prey
And to remind myself
NEVER AGAIN

Simple Words of a Complex Man

Yes it's held together with
Tape and glue and years of pain
But you know what
I can finally see the beauty
In my imperfections
For better or worse
I earned this broken heart
IT IS MINE
And you can't have it back
Not ever

Kevin Schwartzberg

Such a delicate line
And a world of difference
Between
Doing what is right and
Doing the right thing

Simple Words of a Complex Man

Time is supposed to heal all
Bullshit
It feels as fresh as the day it happened
I can still taste the anguish
And hear my pounding heart
This pain
It has no expiration date
And my forgiveness
Will not be rushed

Kevin Schwartzberg

Time marches on
Good or bad
We can't stop the momentum
Small moments
Seemingly insignificant words
A simple smile
Just may change someone's day
Week
Or life
Don't miss that chance
Everyday try to learn a little
And love a lot

Simple Words of a Complex Man

Sometimes all we need
Is that one single moment
To give us the strength
That will change all the rest

Kevin Schwartzberg

Things change faster than we thought possible
Impossible situations become reality
Reality becomes possibility
This minute, this place, this life
We are where we are for a reason
It is time to let go of our need for control
Be brave
Look change square in the face
Curl your lip
And say...
Bring it bitch

Simple Words of a Complex Man

There is no trail of breadcrumbs
Leading me back home
No alter ego for the beast
That dwells within my heart
I don't think there will be
Anymore happy endings
But the longer I live
The more certain I am
We are all stories
Some have just yet to be told

Kevin Schwartzberg

In pain there is an occasion for growth
Out of the darkness comes opportunity
For a stronger and wiser you
This is the true journey of the Phoenix
It steps into the fire not because it seeks death
But because it knows beyond the flames
It will emerge with insight and strength
Spreading a brand new set of wings

Simple Words of a Complex Man

And suddenly an angel stood
Where a man once was
He looked upon the universe
And he whispered thank you
Thank you for reminding me
I have always had wings
And granting me the courage
To use them again

Kevin Schwartzberg

The beauty of this life
Is also the madness of this life
If you choose not to learn
From your mistakes
The universe guarantees
You will get another chance

Simple Words of a Complex Man

Words that desperately need a voice
Are too often the ones left unspoken
The "I love you" you never expressed
Could have been the catalyst for change
You so desperately needed
You will never get this moment back
Trust me when I tell you
Regret is built on the promise of tomorrow
So breathe the fire in your soul
Scream into the night sky
Lead with kindness and passion
Never ever forgetting
The world is empty without your beauty

Kevin Schwartzberg

Soulmates
Twin flames
Call it what you will
We are one in this life
As we have been before
And will be again
Our paths are forever intertwined
There is no possible scenario
No possible universe
Where your very essence
Is not my definition
Of home

To say
Connections like this are rare
Does not begin to explain it
Time and space are irrelevant
Forever lost in the moments since hello
It is clear we knew each other
Before words were even exchanged
Feelings with conversation
Emotions without fear
Even our shadows embraced
Remembering previous intimacy

Kevin Schwartzberg

We don't have to say a word
You know it
I know it
All we need right now
Is today
Let's just get lost in this moment
And worry about tomorrow
If it arrives

Simple Words of a Complex Man

We are desperate for change
Living in our broken past
Constantly comparing ourselves to those
We perceive without imperfection
Rest assured their mirror
Spits the same regret
The same undeniable truth
The only thing constant for everyone
Is hindsight
Until you open your eyes
Accept your past
And live in the now
You will never see
The beauty of your future

Kevin Schwartzberg

We are so much more
Than the decisions we make
Good or bad - right or wrong
Momentary lapses of reason
Do not define the beauty inside
The love that radiates from our souls
The pain that drove us to this place
Remember none of us are perfect
None of us are without blame
Try to be kind to yourself
Trust me
You are worth it

Simple Words of a Complex Man

Yesterday's stories have already been told
Dog eared pages serve as reminders
Of past battles lost and won
Wake up every day with the knowledge
Today is a blank page
Tomorrow can start a new chapter
The novel of your life
Has yet to be written

Kevin Schwartzberg

Time heals everything
Pain fades
Perspectives change
I remember moments
When I thought to myself
This is it
My breaking point
It cannot possibly get any worse
I cannot go on
Now
I wish I could go back
Relive those moments
Knowing that was a vacation
From the hell
I currently reside in
Knowing this too shall pass

Simple Words of a Complex Man

Needle sharp rays of sunlight
Piercing silver lined clouds
Delicate love poems from lonely birds
Carried upon the cool crisp wind
Rapidly running river water
Single mindedly focused on escaping
Icy mountain glaciers
Singing the only song they know
Dew covered blades of grass
Damp and comforting against our skin
Your finger tracing small circles
Upon the sensitive skin of my palm
Tomorrow is never promised
This instant has already passed
Together let's get lost in the moment
Forget all the pain and heartache
Breathe in the beauty
Make today count

Kevin Schwartzberg

You wanted me to believe
I would never be enough
Always alone in a crowd
There was a time
When I looked in the mirror
I could only see your words
But those days are gone
I see love and strength
Compassion and kindness
Most importantly
A man my son is proud of

Simple Words of a Complex Man

It's almost as if I see the words
Escaping from your crimson lips
Unshackled from the dark and complex
Recesses of your malevolent brain
They have one purpose
One purpose only
To further break me
Into the shell of a man
That together we created
But not this time
You don't have that power
I am not that man anymore
After years of keeping my mouth shut
Caught in an emotional purgatory
I have learned the three words
That render you powerless
And will set me free
I
Forgive
You

Kevin Schwartzberg

As poets
As writers
As empaths
Simply as humans
It is our responsibility
Our honor and our obligation
To connect with other hearts
Those who share our love and pain
To hold their hands and fill them with hope
Giving unspoken words to the emotions
They feel have isolated them from the masses
Remember you are not alone my friends
Not by a long shot

Simple Words of a Complex Man

Whatever form it takes
Poetry has a life of its own
Each person consuming
Only what they need
Leaving the rest for others

Kevin Schwartzberg

Poetry is the
Words we write
That our emotions
Dare not speak

Simple Words of a Complex Man

Everyone has poetry inside them
Words just begging to escape
Some of us just have the courage
To rip open our souls
Face the pain head on
Giving life to the words
So you don't have to

Kevin Schwartzberg

The only reason to relive the past
Is to learn how to change the future
The only guarantee we have in life
Is this moment, this second, this day
It's ok to feel sad, hopeless and defeated
These feelings are fleeting and will pass
The sigh of exasperation you just made
Is merely an inhale away from the deep breath
You so desperately need to clear your mind
Most of all...
Never let others fail to see your beauty
Dictate your own self-worth

Simple Words of a Complex Man

One day soon
This will all be in the past
Where you are today
The way you have healed
Seemed almost impossible
Just a short time ago
Never underestimate the power you have
Mountains are conquered
One step at a time
Souls are healed
One breath at a time

Kevin Schwartzberg

Sometimes
For reasons unknown
The universe takes it upon itself
To remind us we are not forsaken
Everything truly happens for a reason
We don't have to carry our burdens alone
There are people out there
Worthy of not only our trust
But our admiration
Strength reveals itself in many ways
And rarely, if ever
Does it pertain to muscles
I am so over feeling exhausted
I am so focused on tomorrow
I have forgotten how to live in the moment
I need to step back and realize
Happiness is not a destination
So much as it is a journey
Small moments of joy
Combine to become an overall
Appreciation for life and what I have

Simple Words of a Complex Man

One day it will just click
You will meet someone
Not how you expect to
Not in the places you are looking
But there they will be
Speaking to your heart
In a language you have
Long since forgotten
This moment...
This person...
Never
Let
Go

Kevin Schwartzberg

The greatest of fears
Often lead to the biggest of revelations
I can't possibly do that
Becomes I can't believe I just did that
I am afraid to fail
Transforms into I fear nothing
There are precious few moments
Within our short fragile lives
Where we can institute change
On such a life altering scale
We just have to have the courage
To stop and take a breath
Grab hold of those moments
And NEVER let go
These are the moments that define us
That enrich our hearts and souls
Reminding us why this life is a gift
Our story has yet to be told
And we get to decide how it ends

Healing
The process is all about me
The result
Is what I choose to share
With everyone else

I refuse to shortchange
Either one of us

Kevin Schwartzberg

A very wise friend told me recently
That time is so precious
There is so very little and
It's gone in the blink of an eye
I believe it is our purpose in each life
To learn something we take to the next
Ultimately we are bound
To find the person who is going
To share in our adventures,
Our growth, and cherish our time and us
If someone is helping us or supporting us
Upon that path, they are meant to be there
If not, they need to find a different path

It really should be that simple.

Simple Words of a Complex Man

Fate is a belief in a power
Other than our own
Fate controls the outcome
Regardless of our desires
Fate excuses us from the guilt
Of taking responsibility for our actions
Since everything happens for a reason
Why not take a chance
Chance is what allows us to dance
Carefree in the grey areas
Chance is the universe leaning
Towards its preferred state of chaos
Chance is the belief that ultimately
We control our own fate

Kevin Schwartzberg

It just takes one brief instant
Sometimes only a few words
To completely change your perspective
What you think you knew
Who you thought someone was
Is suddenly transformed
The careful façade they built
Years of manipulation and pain
Are finally exposed for what they truly were
From that moment forward
You realize you are changed
You evolve
You harness the strength buried within you
You are certain of the path in front of you
And the decisions you made that led you here
They no longer have the ability to hurt you
This moment
This fucking moment
You will never forget it
Or the sensation as you spread your wings
Feel the sun's warmth upon your face
And take that leap

Kevin Schwartzberg

Simple Words of a Complex Man

Words of a Man

Kevin Schwartzberg

I have worked so hard
To build these walls
The idea of life outside them
Is absolutely terrifying

Simple Words of a Complex Man

For years I thought
I was locked behind these walls
All the while never thinking
To try and open the door
The funny thing about walls
We are the architects of their construction
As well as the author of their demolition

Kevin Schwartzberg

I'm jealous of the rain
Lonely droplets of water
Always seeking their own
Regardless of the obstacles
It cannot be stopped
Not stone
Not fire
Not even mountains
Yet here I hide
Behind these walls
Afraid to feel anything

Simple Words of a Complex Man

Lately it seems there is no way
To quiet the voices in my head
Silent screams shaking hands
With vivid technicolor dreams
Always knee deep in the water
Sunlight dancing in your eyes
The waves reflecting your soul
My eyes locked with yours
Afraid to miss a moment

Kevin Schwartzberg

It took me ten years to realize
It would only take me ten seconds
To completely alter the course of my life
Absolute truth and the glorious reality
Of knowing once I speak these words
I will never be the same man again

Simple Words of a Complex Man

I have always known
There are words inside me
Words that need life
Unshackled from pain
Perhaps I should thank you
For completely breaking me
So they could escape

Kevin Schwartzberg

The ink will run dry
Long before my heart has healed

Simple Words of a Complex Man

My past has taught me
That words are the gateway to emotions
Emotions inevitably lead to feelings
And feelings always end with pain
Fuck what they say
I'll take sticks and stones any day
For words can in fact break you

Kevin Schwartzberg

My life is forever changed
For the better with you in it
I truly hope I never have to tell anyone
The story of the woman
Who taught me it was safe to love again
Instead I can simply lean over
Softly kiss your lips
Squeeze your hand
And remember the day we met
When I knew everything had changed

Simple Words of a Complex Man

With reluctant resolve
I can finally accept
We are the single greatest thing
That will never come to pass

Kevin Schwartzberg

Unfortunately my heart has decided
Regardless of your desire to reciprocate

The depth of my love for you
Will never fade

Simple Words of a Complex Man

I love to see you
From the corner of my eye
You don't know I'm watching
So for a moment
You forget to pretend
And the façade fades away
The pain and hurt take a back seat
You finally allow me a glimpse
Of what lies behind your walls
Your laughter is infectious
Everything seems right in the world
Then the moment passes
And like our love
It's a memory
I can never quite seem to hold

Kevin Schwartzberg

After all this time...
The universe connects us again
Certainly this is not our first life together
Nor will it be our last
You would think it would be simple
Like spotting your own face
In a crowded photograph
So why is it
I stand alone again
Always searching...
For a unicorn in a sea of horses

Simple Words of a Complex Man

The only thing that separates
You and I
From being what we know is
Inevitable
Is our willingness to throw
Our lives
Into a complete and utter state
Of chaos
I'm game...are you?

Kevin Schwartzberg

I am haunted by so many things
The smell of you upon my skin
The salty sweet taste of your lips
Even the memory of your voice
Takes me to a familiar place
That no longer feels like home

Simple Words of a Complex Man

I wish I could wash my hands of you
But no matter how hard I scrub
Your fingerprints have stained my soul
And can never be erased

Kevin Schwartzberg

You say I'm distant
Disconnected...
That I live in my own world
You know what, maybe you are right
Maybe I do...
But we both know the reason why don't we
We both know how we arrived here
I have turned the other cheek so many times
I have worn a hole in this carpet
And I am dizzy with regret
Yeah, I think I will stay here
In my own world
Where it is safe
I have learned to prefer this darkness

Simple Words of a Complex Man

Her apathy towards me
Feels disturbingly like home
Although I know I deserve better
She feeds my dysfunction perfectly
It is a never ending struggle
Between my heart and my mind

Kevin Schwartzberg

I push you
You push back
Words that hurt
Spoken with venom
We know them
All too well
Who we were
Acts of kindness
It's all so distant
Lost
In what we have become
At least we have one thing in common

Simple Words of a Complex Man

Maybe all of this
My pain
Your pain
It all happened for a reason
Without that agony
You and I
Would have never spoken a word
We would exist on the same planet
Under the same sky
Never truly understanding
The astounding beauty that could be us

Kevin Schwartzberg

I don't need to be **perfect**

    I just need to be perfect *for you*

Simple Words of a Complex Man

I'm not sure if I am more terrified of being alone
Or continuing to live this bullshit façade
We call love

Kevin Schwartzberg

I am alone again
Missing your presence
A stranger to myself
The lone survivor
Of my heart's massacre
I have been here before
This too shall pass
Lonely is something I know well

Simple Words of a Complex Man

You think you know me
You do not
Nobody really does
I desperately want you to know
The man behind the walls
Tied up and terrified
Hiding behind all these fancy words
Although my shackles may be velvet
Have no illusions
They bind as tightly as chains
They just lack the courtesy
To admit their true intentions

Kevin Schwartzberg

You stand atop your ivory tower
Looking down upon the universe
All the while never realizing
The universe will always be
Looking down upon you
Remember my dear
We are all angels
We all have wings
Some of us just have the courage
To take that first leap
Before we remember how to fly

Kevin Schwartzberg

I miss you
I miss your laugh
I miss your eyes
I miss your body
But more than anything
I miss how I feel around you
You feel like home

Simple Words of a Complex Man

Every teardrop that falls
Is a silent tribute to the life
That could have been
The time we had together
The laughter we shared
They are never lost
Your face is my waking dream
Your embrace holds me while I sleep
I'd like to think I built these walls
To keep others out
But the truth is
I'm trying to keep you in

Kevin Schwartzberg

There is something about
Another person's heartbeat
Gently tapping on your chest
Warm breath soft upon your neck
Followed by gentle butterfly kisses
Sex is everywhere we turn
But synchronized moments
Of real connection
That is what my soul craves

Simple Words of a Complex Man

So many people talk and talk
Covering up their discomfort
Meaningless words strung together
To hide their own self doubt
I want to just be with someone
To share their time and space
Never having to exchange a word
All the while knowing
This is what love sounds like

Kevin Schwartzberg

For all of us who choose compassion
Who love with everything we have
Who desire to see the good in others
Always turning the other cheek and smiling
Beware
There are those that will seek us out
Wanting only to devour our kindness

Simple Words of a Complex Man

I have spent my lifetime
Striving for moments of excellence
All the while failing to realize
The beauty in perfected mediocrity

Kevin Schwartzberg

I have learned it is best to
Keep everyone at arm's length
It greatly reduces the likelihood
Of them seeing in me
What I feel about myself

Simple Words of a Complex Man

I can't even remember now
Did I stumble and fall
Or did I just collapse to my knees
I vividly recall the tears though
Filling my eyes
Obscuring my vision
My hands wrapped around my head
That awful scream of anguish
Then the calm
It was in that moment I evolved
I will NEVER be this broken again

Kevin Schwartzberg

I have known this same pain
For my entire life
It's the faces
That tend to blur together

Simple Words of a Complex Man

I put so much weight
On who and what I used to be
Holding onto the past
I never stopped to realize
I am now the evolution
Of that man

Kevin Schwartzberg

He is sleepless nights
Struggling with memories past
The smell of warm coffee
And breakfast in bed
He is tear-inducing conversations
Moments of unexplainable depth
And inappropriate bursts of laughter
He is deep, slow, passionate kisses
Designed to steal your breath
And leave you begging for more
He is a soulful embrace
Riddled with love
And wracked with agony
He is fearless in the face of enemies
And terrified of what lives within
But most of all
He is a work in progress
A slayer of demons
And I promise he is worth the wait

Simple Words of a Complex Man

I have only one heart
The one you see before you now
The very same one I exposed
The day we first met
And every day since then
It is not perfect
Not be any means
But it beats with a fierce intensity
As loyal as they come
Yours for the taking
For reasons I am not yet clear of
I feel safe placing it in your hands
Please be gentle

Kevin Schwartzberg

I promise to always treat you
The way that I wish
You would treat yourself

Simple Words of a Complex Man

You always ask why I'm quiet
You want to know what I'm thinking
After a pause I say
Nothing
But we both know that's not true
I just don't have the words
How do I explain everything
Every touch
Every taste
Every moment
I want to memorize every single detail
So even if you leave with my heart
I will always have tonight

Kevin Schwartzberg

I don't need over the top
Gestures of love and devotion
Just the simple knowledge
I am cherished
To actually feel desired
To feel the warmth
Of another person's energy
And to know I am enough

Simple Words of a Complex Man

You see me as a stoic
An immovable stone in the storm
I have learned to wear that mask
The art of self-preservation
Perfected from perceived necessity
There are however a precious few
That I let see the anguish
See through the walls of sarcasm
The carefully crafted words of bravery
For them I allow my façade to break
As my heart breaks daily
I don't need answers
I don't need you to fix it
I just need to share my tears
Pour myself into your hands
Hear you tell me it will be ok
And know you will hold me
Until I can breathe again

Kevin Schwartzberg

She said
You seem broken
Solemn and defeated
As if she could read my heart
Suddenly the man with all the fancy words
Was speechless
You want to know if I'm broken...
Honestly I'm not sure
I have been this way for so long
It is the only truth I know
Maybe we are all broken
We are simply waiting
For someone to notice

The curse of being an empath
People will often unburden their soul
By placing it upon yours

Kevin Schwartzberg

I cannot be anything to anyone
Until I am everything to myself

Simple Words of a Complex Man

You taught me what it means
To be a father first
You always lead by example
Never just with empty words
Always my biggest fan
Often from the sidelines
With no recognition
The voice of reason
Even when I refused to listen
Looking back now I realize
You have always been my rock
Together we created
The man before you today

Kevin Schwartzberg

I want the ones with scars
Those who have overcome adversity
Who have walked through the fire
Who know the feel of the flames
Dancing upon their skin
And don't fear the change it brings
Give me what others see as
The broken souls
These are my people
The ones that feel too much
That love with all they are
Embracing the pain they have earned
These are the ones I want by my side
The ones with scars

Simple Words of a Complex Man

My words may not
Always express
The depth of my
Emotions
But my heart speaks
Loud and clear
To those who care to
Listen

Kevin Schwartzberg

My walls are becoming windows
I can clearly see the beauty outside
I want to smash the glass
Let the cold crisp air in
Breathe it deep into my heart
Cleansing my soul
But healing takes time
Please be patient - I am worth the wait

Simple Words of a Complex Man

What if I told you
You make me re-evaluate
The definition of love
Would you understand
Would you know
How much fear
I had to overcome
To even share this with you
I have worked so hard
To erect these walls
The idea of life outside them
Is absolutely terrifying

Kevin Schwartzberg

I want an emotional and spiritual connection
Chills delivered by a simple touch
Heartbeats that fall naturally in sync
Uncontrollable laughter
And comfortable silence

Simple Words of a Complex Man

I love you
So easy to say
Casually spoken words
Devoid of all meaning
However
The three little words
I really need to feel

You
Are
Enough

Kevin Schwartzberg

Of all the gifts
You could have given me
Of all the things
I thought I wanted
You gave me the one thing
I so desperately needed
And had no idea existed
Without you
I never would have found
The 10 seconds of courage
That changed my life
Thank you hardly seems enough
And I'm not sure how to gift-wrap
Everlasting appreciation

Simple Words of a Complex Man

Every sunrise brings redemption
Every sunset brings reflection
What did I learn
Was I kind
Did I make a positive impact
In another person's day
I am a work in progress
But I want you to be proud
I want to be the man everyone sees
For once I just want to believe
I am enough

Kevin Schwartzberg

Yes
I am broken
But I have learned to embrace it
My broken shards create a mosaic
Of who and what I am today
I now choose to surround myself
With the rare souls that see
The beauty contained within these pieces
Who accept me at face value
Who continue to show me
Love will always exist within me

Kevin Schwartzberg

Simple Words of a Complex Man

Nobody ever laid on his or her deathbed
Thinking I loved too much
I didn't work enough
Or I laughed too hard
So live each day
Like tomorrow may never come
Smile when you really want to cry
Dance in the rain
And love like a motherfucker

Kevin Schwartzberg

Acknowledgements

To: My dad, who has always been my rock and my example of what a man should be. Thank you for always filling me with the drive to be better, a never ending supply of laughter, and for teaching me the fine art of the F bomb. I love you Pop.

To: My mothers, some people don't even have one mother in their life. I was lucky enough to have two. I love you both.

To: My family close and far, it has been a rough couple years. I wouldn't have gotten through it without your love and encouragement. Bockstar!

To: The writers who have been not only my guides in this world of poetry, but my friends. There are too many to name, and I love you all. But, I feel the need to thank a few personally. Steph, I would have never shared a word without your friendship and support. Alfa, this book simply would not exist without you. Thank you for all the chats, calls, and proof reading,

And most importantly: All my readers and supporters on Facebook and Instagram. Thank you doesn't begin to describe how I feel. I appreciate you all giving me the opportunity to share my emotions with you. This is for you.

About the Author

Kevin writes with the knowledge and emotion of someone who has been through hell and back. A single father who has always worn his heart on his sleeve, Kevin carries pain in his veins and hope in his heart. He learned at a young age that words have the power to both hurt and heal. He spent many years writing in secret, but life has a way of causing the dam to break, and all those emotions could no longer be contained. His words stem from life experience, both good and bad, and he weaves all that darkness and light into lines that stir the soul.

A wonderful contributor to the online poetry community, Kevin also shares his words on both Facebook and Instagram. When he is not writing, he can be found spending time with his awesome son or indulging his passion for photography. He currently resides just outside of Chicago with his son and his two sphynx cats, Arya and Fiona.

You can find more of his words on social media:

Instagram: @simple_words_of_a_complex_man

Facebook: facebook.com/simplewordsofacomplexman

www.ingramcontent.com/pod-product-compliance
Lightning Source LLC
Chambersburg PA
CBHW021949290426
44108CB00012B/1007